Workshop on Computational Models of Spatial Language Interpretation and Generation 2013

(CoSLI-3)

Held at the 10th International Conference on Computational Semantics (IWCS 2013)

Potsdam, Germany
19 March 2013

ISBN: 978-1-62748-401-5

Printed from e-media with permission by:

Curran Associates, Inc.
57 Morehouse Lane
Red Hook, NY 12571

Some format issues inherent in the e-media version may also appear in this print version.

Printed by Curran Associates, Inc. (2013)

Association for Computational Linguistics
209 N. Eighth Street
Stroudsburg, Pennsylvania 18360

Phone: 1-570-476-8006
Fax: 1-570-476-0860

acl@aclweb.org

Additional copies of this publication are available from:

Curran Associates, Inc.
57 Morehouse Lane
Red Hook, NY 12571 USA
Phone: 845-758-0400
Fax: 845-758-2634
Email: curran@proceedings.com
Web: www.proceedings.com

TABLE OF CONTENTS

Spatial Descriptions in Type Theory with Records

Simon Dobnik and Robin Cooper

Department of Philosophy, Linguistics and Theory of Science
University of Gothenburg, Box 200, 405 30 Göteborg, Sweden
{simon.dobnik@,robin.cooper@ling}.gu.se
http://www.flov.gu.se

Abstract. We present how TTR (Type Theory with Records) can model both geometric perception and conceptual (world) knowledge relating to the meaning of spatial descriptions for a robotic agent.

1 Introduction

TTR [2,3] is a type theory with records which leads to a view of meaning which is tightly linked to perception and classification. An agent makes *judgements* that an object a (an individual or a situation) is of type T (written as $a : T$). The notion of truth is related to such judgements. A type T is "true" just in case there is something a such that $a : T$. However, types are independent of their extensions (also known as *proof objects* or *witnesses*), for example, an agent may know a type but not its extension or two agents may disagree about the extension of a type. An agent learns judgements through his interaction with its environment and other agents. The type systems that agents develop converge to a common standard through constant refinements.

Types are either basic or complex (that is constructed from components). Examples of basic types in this paper are *Ind* and *Real* whose witnesses are individuals and real numbers respectively. Examples of complex types are types constructed from predicates and arguments (*p-types*) such as left(a,b) (intuitively the type of situation where a is to the left of b) and *record types* such as $\begin{bmatrix} \text{a}:\mathit{Ind} \\ \text{b}:\mathit{Ind} \\ \text{c}_{\text{left}}:\text{left(a,b)} \end{bmatrix}$. Record types are sets of fields, pairs which consist of a label (represented to the left of the ':') and a type (to the right). There may not be two fields with the same label. A witness for this record type will be a record with fields with the same labels and witnesses of the corresponding type (and possibly also additional fields with other unique labels). Labels with a 'c' are used here where the type is a p-type (intuitively a constraint on the objects in the record). Such types are often *dependent* in that they are constructed from objects in other fields of the record being judged.

Type theory is attractive as a theory for relating perception to higher level conceptual reasoning because it is based on the notion of judging objects to be of types which can be regarded as an abstract theory of perception. Thus it provides us with a theory that encompasses both low-level perception and high-level semantic reasoning in a way that is not usual in standard linguistic approaches to formal semantics. Thus it offers the possibility of connecting the kind of work in implementations of perception by robots to high level semantics. It is frequently not trivial to connect models of robot perception to natural language semantics in a systematic way (for an approach see [13]). Furthermore, by keeping linguistic and perceptual meaning representations in separate modules their interaction can be hard to explore. We are attempting to bridge this gap.

We attempt to illustrate this approach by sketching how this type theory might model how spatial relations can be generated by a mobile agent's perception of its environment. We show how types representing geometric knowledge required for the meaning representations of spatial descriptions are built from sensory observations (perceptual knowledge). We also demonstrate how perceptual types interact with linguistic type representations (conceptual knowledge). Our aim here is not to say anything new about either sensory perception or about the semantic analysis of the semantics of spatial expression but to give some idea of how both could be comprehended in a single theory.

2 Representing robot states and updates

We can do little more here than indicate some of the types involved and how they are related to each other. See [6] for a more detailed proposal concerning how robot learning might be modelled. We will use types to model the partial information that the robot has about the state that it is in. The type of the initial state of the robot may be:

$$
\begin{array}{l}
\mathit{InitRobotState} = \\
\left[\begin{array}{lll}
\text{self} & : & \left[\begin{array}{lll}
\text{a} & : & \mathit{Ind} \\
\text{pnt} = \left[\begin{array}{lll} \text{x} & = & 0 \\ \text{y} & = & 0 \end{array}\right] & : & \mathit{Point} \\
\text{orient}=0 & : & \mathit{Real} \\
c_{\text{point}} & : & \text{observed\_point(self.pnt)} \\
c_{\text{loc}} & : & \text{located(self.a,self.pnt)}
\end{array}\right] \\
c_{\text{robot}} & : & \text{robot(self.a)} \\
\text{pm} = [\text{self.pnt}] & : & \mathit{PointMap} \\
\text{objects}=[\text{self}] & : & [\mathit{Object}(\text{pm})] \\
c_{\text{object\_map}} & : & \text{obj\_map(objects, pm)} \\
\text{beliefs}=[] & : & \mathit{RecType} \\
\text{time}=0 & : & \mathit{Time}
\end{array}\right]
\end{array}
$$

The 'self'-field requires a record corresponding to a located individual, a point in (two-dimensional) space represented as a record with fields for the x- and y-coordinates (initially set to 0), an orientation represented as a real number, initially 0, and two constraints which require that the robot has observed the point at which it is located.

The notation *label=value:Type* used in the 'pnt' and 'orient' fields here is known as a *manifest field* and is used to represent a field *label:*$Type_{value}$, where the $Type_{value}$ is a restriction of *Type* so that its unique witness is *value*. The 'pm'-field is for a point map modelled as a list of points, initially the singleton list containing the location of 'self'. The point map is a list of individuated point landmarks as built with a SLAM procedure [5] . The 'objects'-field is for a list of objects assembled from the point map (that is, an object map based on 'pm'), initially the singleton list containing 'self'. This is an object map. As the robot moves around it discovers new landmarks which are added to the point map and their estimate of global location (relative to the robot's origin) is continuously improved. Since at this point no point landmarks have been discovered yet, the list of objects built from these landmarks, and the list of beliefs about these objects is also empty. At the time $t+1$ the agent may transition to a new state by moving and making new observations. It may also hear an utterance made by its conversational partner.

SLAM gives us a geometric representation of the environment containing abstracted point landmarks in a global coordinate frame from which angles and distances required for geometric representation of spatial descriptions can be determined [10,12,14]. The robot's list of objects represented in the 'objects'-field of the state are located at points and regions within this point map. A geometric representation of a region or a volume consists of a group of 2-dimensional points from the point map that can be hulled with a convex hull.

The types *PointObject* and *RegionObject* are relative to a point map, and this is represented by functions returning a type (dependent types):

$$PointObject = \lambda p{:}PointMap(\begin{bmatrix} \text{a} & : & Ind \\ \text{pnt} & : & Point \\ \text{orient} & : & Real \\ \text{c}_{\text{point}} & : & \text{observed\_point}(\text{pnt},p) \\ \text{c}_{\text{loc}} & : & \text{located}(\text{a},\text{pnt}) \end{bmatrix})$$

$$RegionObject = \lambda p{:}PointMap(\begin{bmatrix} \text{a} & : & Ind \\ \text{reg} & : & PointMap \\ \text{orient} & : & Real \\ \text{c}_{\text{region}} & : & \text{region}(\text{reg},p) \\ \text{c}_{\text{loc}} & : & \text{located}(\text{a},\text{reg}) \end{bmatrix})$$

$$Object = \lambda p{:}PointMap(PointObject(p) \vee RegionObject(p))$$

(See [6, p.8] for a characterization of the predicates 'observed_point' and 'region'.) Once the robot has identified located objects in this way it can compute spatial relations between these objects by comparing their 'pnt' (location point) or 'reg' (location region) fields. Beliefs about such spatial relations, coded by p-types) will be added to the 'beliefs'-field in the robot state.

3 Representing spatial relations

Geometrically, the spatial relation 'to the left of'[1] holds between three individuals conceptualised as objects of type *RegionObject*: the located object, the reference object and the viewpoint which determines the orientation of the reference frame [7,9]. If o_1, o_2, o_3:*RegionObject* and f_{relation} is a spatial relation classifier[2] of type *Region→Region→Orientation→Type* then

e:left(o_1.a,o_2.a,o_3.a) iff $e : f_{\text{relation}}(o_1.\text{reg}, o_2.\text{reg}, o_3.\text{orient})$
and $f_{\text{relation}}(o_1.\text{reg}, o_2.\text{reg}, o_3.\text{orient}) = \text{left}_{geom}(o_1.\text{reg}, o_2.\text{reg}, o_3.\text{orient})$.

Two relativisations or transformations of region locations must be performed before the classification can take place (both of which can be expressed in our formalism): (i) the (global) coordinate frame must be rotated to correspond to the orientation of o_3; and (ii) the origin of the global coordinate frame must be transposed so that it is identical to the centre point of the region of location of o_2 (cf. [11]). Since o_1's region of location has been relativised we only need to learn one classifier function regardless of the viewpoint. The TTR representation allows us to combine perceptual classification with qualitative spatial representation [1].

The new belief [e:left(o_1.a,o_2.a,o_3.a)] is merged with the robot's beliefs in the 'beliefs'-field of the robot state and can be used, for example to answer a question about the location of o_1.[3]

The influence of world knowledge on the semantics of the spatial descriptions goes beyond conceptualisation of objects. For example, [4] describe experiments involving pictures of a man holding an umbrella at various angles and with various degrees of exposure to rain presented to human observers and conclude that for the spatial relation 'over' the satisfaction of the constraint 'umbrella provides protection from rain' is more than 'the umbrella is within the geometric spatial template for 'over'. A predicate representing 'over' would obey something like the following conditional (not biconditional):

$$e\text{:over}(o_1.\text{a},o_2.\text{a},o_3.\text{a}) \text{ if } e\text{:}\begin{bmatrix} \text{c}_{\text{rain}} & : & \text{rain}(o_3.\text{a}) \\ \text{c}_{\text{umbrella}} & : & \text{umbrella}(o_2.\text{a}) \\ \text{c}_{\text{over}_{\text{geom}}} & : & \text{over}_{geom}(o_2.\text{vol},o_1.\text{vol}) \\ \text{c}_{\text{protects}} & : & \text{protects}(o_3.\text{a},o_1.\text{a},o_2.\text{a}) \end{bmatrix}$$

where o_1, o_2 and o_3 are of type *VolumeObject* similar to *RegionObject* except that three dimensional volumes are used rather than two dimensional regions.

Geometrically ($\text{c}_{\text{over}_{\text{geom}}}$), the umbrella must be in a particular spatial configuration with the man which can be trained as a classifier . 'over_{geom}' is typically not susceptible to perspective shifts as the viewpoint is fixed by the gravity and hence the third object that would determine the viewpoint is not necessary. Hence, before the classification

[1] We are considering the relative notion here, not that which is based on the intrinsic orientation of some object which has a front and a back.

[2] See [8] for a TTR account of classifier learning from human interaction.

[3] Objects o_2 and o_3 would have to be selected separately beforehand. The reference object o_2 should be some contextually salient object. The viewpoint object o_3 should be the agreed viewpoint in the discourse.

takes place only the origin of the global coordinate frame must be transposed to the centre point of the volume of location of o_2.

The constraint c_{protects} represents a conceptual constraint on witnesses of the ptype over(o_1.a, o_2.a, o_3.a) where the ptype protects(o_3, o_1, o_2) may in its turn also rely on a perceptual classifier. What is important here is that this constraint can have been learned by the agent not through perceptual observation but through linguistic communication, for example by being explicitly told that protection from the rain is required. Alternatively it could have been learned by hypothesising this fact after observing situations of humans, umbrellas and rain. Through reasoning humans are able to create increasingly more abstract types which are ultimately grounded in perception[4]. In our view there is no clear cut-off point between low level perceptual knowledge and high-level conceptual knowledge as traditionally assumed.

Since we assume that the geometric meaning constraint $c_{\text{over}_{\text{geom}}}$ is determined by a probabilistic classifier, the acceptable deviations of the umbrella from the prototypical vertical upright position and their gradience are accounted for. The representation predicts that a situation where a man holds an umbrella in the upright position and therefore the $c_{\text{over}_{\text{geom}}}$ constraint is defined with high probability but the umbrella does not provide protection from the rain cannot have the denotation of the ptype over(o_3,o_1,o_2) since the constraint c_{protects} is not satisfied. Since ptypes such as over(o_3,o_1,o_2) may be characterised by probabilistic knowledge as well, we could regard all constraints as expressing a degree of belief that particular situations are of particular types (see [6, p.17–18] for more details and also probabilistic TTR [in prep.]).

4 Conclusion and further work

We have presented a brief sketch how TTR can be used to represent different meaning components of spatial descriptions. Its strengths are that it considers meaning representations to be based on perception and that it can represent different meaning modalities in a unified way. It thus bridges the gap between models of natural language and models of perception. In such a model it becomes transparent that there are many similarities in the way an agent learns and applies the meanings of linguistic and non linguistic representations. Being a formal computational model it is well suited for modelling language and perception in artificial agents which will be the focus of our work in the future.

Acknowledgements We thank 3 anonymous reviewers of the CoSLI 3 workshop for their valuable comments. We would also like to thank Staffan Larsson for important discussion in connection with this work.

References

1. Cohn, A.G., Renz, J.: Qualitative spatial representation and reasoning. In: Frank van Harmelen, V.L., Porter, B. (eds.) Handbook of Knowledge Representation, Foundations of Artificial Intelligence, vol. 3, chap. 13, pp. 551–596. Elsevier (2008)

[4] Although we do not, of course, claim that all types are grounded in physical perception

2. Cooper, R.: Austinian truth, attitudes and type theory. Research on Language and Computation 3(2), 333–362 (2005)
3. Cooper, R.: Type theory and semantics in flux. In: Kempson, R., Asher, N., Fernando, T. (eds.) Handbook of the Philosophy of Science, General editors: Dov M Gabbay, Paul Thagard and John Woods, vol. 14. Elsevier BV (2012)
4. Coventry, K.R., Prat-Sala, M., Richards, L.: The interplay between geometry and function in the apprehension of Over, Under, Above and Below. Journal of memory and language 44(3), 376–398 (2001)
5. Dissanayake, M.W.M.G., Newman, P.M., Durrant-Whyte, H.F., Clark, S., Csorba, M.: A solution to the simultaneous localization and map building (SLAM) problem. IEEE Transactions on Robotic and Automation 17(3), 229–241 (2001)
6. Dobnik, S., Cooper, R., Larsson, S.: Modelling language, action, and perception in type theory with records (January 2013), `http://sites.google.com/site/typetheorywithrecords/drafts/perceptual-ttr-post-proceedings.pdf`, manuscript
7. Herskovits, A.: Language and spatial cognition: an interdisciplinary study of the prepositions in English. Cambridge University Press, Cambridge (1986)
8. Larsson, S.: The TTR perceptron: Dynamic perceptual meanings and semantic coordination. In: Artstein, R., Core, M., DeVault, D., Georgila, K., Kaiser, E., Stent, A. (eds.) SemDial 2011 (Los Angelogue): Proceedings of the 15th Workshop on the Semantics and Pragmatics of Dialogue. pp. 140–148. Los Angeles, California (September 21—23 2011)
9. Levinson, S.C.: Space in language and cognition: explorations in cognitive diversity. Cambridge University Press, Cambridge (2003)
10. Logan, G.D., Sadler, D.D.: A computational analysis of the apprehension of spatial relations. In: Bloom, P., Peterson, M.A., Nadel, L., Garrett, M.F. (eds.) Language and Space, pp. 493–530. MIT Press, Cambridge, MA (1996)
11. Maillat, D.: The semantics and pragmatics of directionals: a case study in English and French. Ph.D. thesis, Committee for Comparative Philology and General Linguistics, University of Oxford, Oxford, UK (May 2003)
12. Regier, T., Carlson, L.A.: Grounding spatial language in perception: an empirical and computational investigation. Journal of Experimental Psychology: General 130(2), 273–298 (2001)
13. Roy, D.: Semiotic schemas: a framework for grounding language in action and perception. Artificial Intelligence 167(1-2), 170–205 (Sep 2005)
14. Zwarts, J., Winter, Y.: Vector space semantics: A model-theoretic analysis of locative prepositions. Journal of Logic, Language and Information 9, 169–211 (2000)

Deriving Salience Models from Human Route Directions

Jana Götze and Johan Boye

KTH, School of Computer Science and Communication, 100 44 Stockholm, Sweden

Abstract. We present an approach to derive individual preferences in the use of landmarks for route instructions in a city environment.[1] Each possible landmark that a person can refer to in a given situation is modelled as a feature vector, and the preference (or *salience*) associated with the landmark can be computed as a weighted sum of these features. The weight vector, representing the person's personal salience model, is automatically derived from the person's own route descriptions. Experiments show that the derived salience models can correctly predict the user's choice of landmark in 69% of the cases.

1 Introduction

Automatically providing real-time route instructions to city pedestrians is an increasingly important problem, as more and more people have smartphones with GPS receivers. Such wayfinding systems use data from a geographic database to construct a route from the user's starting position to his stated goal, and then give the instructions as the user is moving: When the user reaches a node p_i in the planned route, the system informs the user how he should go to get to the next node p_{i+1}. Obviously, it is vital that each instruction is unambiguous and understandable, lest the user takes a wrong turn.

It would be preferable if wayfinding systems would base their instructions on *landmarks*, by which we understand distinctive objects in the city environment, since it is well established that it is predominantly by landmarks people describe routes to one another (see e.g. [2]). However, even on this basic premise, there are a number of options to consider. At each decision point, there are a number of possible landmarks to choose from, and which one(s) to use in a specific route instruction is a difficult problem. In the literature, it is generally assumed that the candidate landmarks can be assigned a *salience* measure, by which they can be compared, and the most salient features are also the most suitable to use in route descriptions. Many researchers have proposed schemes for computing salience from a variety of factors (see e.g. [3, 6, 9]).

In this article, we investigate to what extent salience computations can be data-driven, that is, (semi-)automatically estimated from human route descriptions. Our aim is to create empirically motivated *personalized* salience models, and integrate them into our spoken-dialogue system for city exploration [1]. Two

[1] Supported by the European Commission, project *Spacebook*, grant no 270019.

hypotheses underlie our work: Firstly, that salience is *user-dependent*. Secondly, if a user is asked to give a routing instruction in a specific situation, he would do so using the landmarks he himself thinks are most salient.

The second hypothesis suggests a kind of tuning mechanism for a wayfinding system: Before being guided by the system, the user first walks around and describes the way he is going by means of landmarks. The system interprets the user's descriptions and uses them to derive a personalized salience model, which can later be used when guiding the same user in other parts of the city. The present paper presents a preliminary study showing that this idea is indeed viable.

2 Deriving Salience Models

For the learning of salience models, we use the Large Margin Algorithm, introduced in [4]. Each landmark can be described as a vector of numerical features, $\mathbf{x} = (x_1, \ldots, x_n)$ specifying costs along n dimensions. The dimensions might represent scalar attributes such as distance, or categorical attributes (e.g. 1 if the landmark is a restaurant, 0 if it is not). The salience $s(\mathbf{x})$ is a linear combination $\mathbf{w} \cdot \mathbf{x}$, where $\mathbf{w} = (w_1, \ldots, w_n)$ is the salience model that specifies the relative importance of the different features for the user. Naturally we do not assume that the user knows the values of his salience model, or indeed even that such a model exists. Instead we automatically infer the model as follows:

Whenever a person uses a landmark A in a description, he is preferring A over a number of other candidates that *could have been* used in the description but were not. That is to say that A has a lower cost according to the person's personal salience model than has any other candidate B, i.e. $\mathbf{w} \cdot (\mathbf{x_B} - \mathbf{x_A}) > 0$, where $\mathbf{x_A}$ and $\mathbf{x_B}$ are the vectors representing A, and B, respectively. Each route description from the user involving a landmark thus generates a number of inequalities, all in the form $\mathbf{w} \cdot (\mathbf{x_{B_i}} - \mathbf{x_{A_i}}) > 0$, for $1 \leq i \leq m$. Our goal is to find appropriate values for the weights in $\mathbf{w}$ that satisfy all these inequalities. This can be done by solving the following linear optimization problem, e.g. with the Simplex method [7]:

$$\begin{array}{lll} \text{minimize} & \sum_{j=1}^{n} w_j & \\ \text{subject to} & \mathbf{w} \cdot (\mathbf{x_{B_i}} - \mathbf{x_{A_i}}) \geq 1, & 1 \leq i \leq m \\ & w_j \geq 0, & 1 \leq j \leq n \end{array}$$

This formulation of the problem assumes that a person is always consistent in his preferences. For the case he is not, we use a slightly extended version of the basic Large Margin Algorithm (see [4] for details).

3 Problem Description and Encoding

Consider the example in Figure 3. The figure shows a situation in one of our experiments where the subject chooses to describe the way using a supermarket,

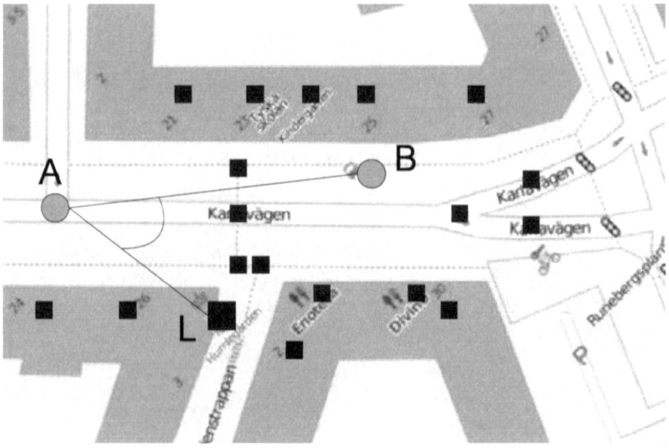

Fig. 1. An example route segment from A to B. The squares represent the landmarks in the contexts of A and B. L represents a landmark referred to by the user (a supermarket).

indicated by the larger square: *"and then when you've reached a crossroad [...] you turn to your left and you'll see there's gonna be an* ICA, *a foodstore, and a little bit further down the road there's gonna be a bus stop"*. In the figure, the "crossroad" is indicated by "A", and the bus stop by "B".

Every landmark belongs to the *context* of its closest node. When describing the way from A (the *starting node* of the segment) to B (the *goal* node of the segment), all landmarks in the contexts of these two nodes are possible referents. We will refer to this set of landmarks as the *candidate set* for A and B. This set is visualized as square-shaped icons in the figures. The candidate set is obtained from the OpenStreetMap (OSM) geographic database [5].

The method described in Section 2 requires every landmark L to which the user can refer to be modelled as a vector of features. In this experiment, we use a vector of 12 features that are computable from our geographic database. These features form an initial set of structural landmark features [8] and we are planning to further explore which other features are important for computing salience. The features used here are the following:

- **Distance** between the user's position A and the landmark L.
- **Distance** between the landmark L and the goal node B.
- **Angle** between the lines AL and AB.
- **Name**: Categorial attribute having the value 1 if the landmark has a name (e.g. "7-Eleven"), or belongs to something that has a name, e.g. a node on X street, and 0 otherwise.
- **Type**: These 8 features represent the type of the landmark according to whether they belong into the categories *road network*, i.e. the landmark node is part of a street, *building*, *eating & pleasure*, e.g. a restaurant or a theater,

shops, *entrances*, i.e. a specific house number on a street, *areas*, e.g. a park or a construction site, *structures*, e.g. a statue or a fountain, or *other*. Each landmark is of at least one type, which is indicated by the value 1 in the corresponding slot.

In the example in Figure 3, the supermarket that is referenced by the user (the larger square), is represented by the vector $(5.0, 5.0, 40, 1, 0, 0, 0, 1, 0, 0, 0, 0)$. The first two positions contain the distances (the 2-logarithm of the actual distance in metres, rounded to the nearest integer). The third position represents the angle (in degrees). The '1' in the succeeding slot indicates that the landmark has a name "ICA". The values in the final 8 slots indicate that the landmark is a shop, but no other type.

4 Data Collection

A number of subjects (engineering students) were asked to describe a route to someone unfamiliar with the area, imagining that they were talking to this person on the phone. The subjects had just walked the same route themselves and should therefore remember it well. To further help them recall their trajectory, they were also shown their route on a map on the screen by a moving mouse cursor (i.e. without using speech), and they could also look at the map while they described the route.

The subjects' speech was recorded and segmented according to route segments before transcription. Each route segment starts at a node A and ends at a goal node B. The nodes A and B were inferred from the subjects' instructions, as they used phrases like *"and when you are at the intersection, turn left and walk until the bus stop"*. While the route as a whole differed only slightly from subject to subject, the routes do not necessarily consist of the same number of segments. The segmentation here is derived from the subjects' descriptions. Each segment was also annotated with all landmarks in the database that the subject referred to. The set of landmarks used by the subjects often includes the goal node B itself, as in the example in Figure 3. In that example, the instruction was annotated with the node representing the supermarket and the node representing the bus stop. It can also be the case that the goal node B is not mentioned explicitly, as in *"and when you are at the traffic light, cross street S"*. In this case, the goal node B is implicit, and not part of the landmarks referred to by the subject.

Prior to describing the route, the subjects had walked them themselves, following instructions given by our prototype system. This means that their own instructions might be influenced by what they just heard. However, the system's instructions only partly used landmarks and otherwise relied on relative instructions such as "turn left". This strategy sometimes resulted in ambiguous or wrong instructions, and the subjects were asked to "improve upon the system's behavior".

For each subject, we thus have a number of annotated segments, each consisting of a start node, an end node, and at least one landmark that the subject referred to (his *preferred* landmark(s) in this segment). Segments where the subject didn't refer to anything at all were excluded from this experiment. The candidate set for the segment (i.e. the landmarks the user *could have* referred to) was automatically computed from the OSM database and contains on average 22 landmarks.

The preferred landmarks might or might not be part of the candidate set. There are two possible reasons for a preferred landmark not to be part of the candidate set: Either the user referred to something that is not in the database at all (in which case we removed the reference), or he referred to something that is farther away, and doesn't belong to the context of neither A nor B (this latter case actually never happened in our experiments).

An *instance*, of the salience model learning problem, then, is a candidate set together with one or several preferred landmarks, at least one of which is part of the candidate set. The set of all instances for a particular user was split into a training set and a test set. The training set was used to derive a salience model **w** according to the method presented in Section 2. To evaluate **w**, the salience of each member of each instance of the test set was computed. A *successful* instance is one in which one of the preferred landmarks had the best salience according to **w**. The number of successful instances in the test set is an indicator of how well the learned salience model actually reflects the preferences of the user.

5 Results

The results are presented in Table 1. For all individual salience models, at least half of the test instances are successful. In one case, the model even returns all the instances as successful. To get an insight into how well the models perform on those landmarks that did not receive the lowest cost but were used by the subject, we also compute the measure RANK. For this measure, we compute the percentage of landmarks receiving costs that were equal or higher than the preferred landmark's cost (recall that the lower the cost, the more salient the landmark). The number of landmarks that can be referred to differs depending on the particular route segment and this measure reflects how high the salience model ranked a landmark in comparison to all available landmarks. For example, subject 1's model has two successful test instances, and in the other two ranks the preferred landmark as 3 of 14 in one instance, and as 5 of 39 in the other.

6 Discussion

The results are encouraging insofar that in 69%, the method actually managed to mimic the user's own salience preferences, although the model is built from very few training examples. Note that the ratio of training vs. testing segments differs between the subjects. Initially, the training set contains two thirds of the route segments. For some subjects, the training size had to be reduced, because our algorithm is limited in the number and size of route segments it can process.

Table 1. For evaluation, we used the induced weights to compute costs on test sets and counted in how many cases the best option was a landmark used by the subject, including also reference to streets and squares. SEGMENTS: total number of route segments, TESTS: number of test instances, SUCC: number (and percentage) of successful test instances, RANK: percentage of landmarks with equal or higher cost

SUBJ	SEGMENTS	TESTS	SUCC	RANK
1	13	4	2 (0.50)	0.93
2	16	5	3 (0.60)	0.94
3	9	3	2 (0.67)	0.94
4	9	3	2 (0.67)	0.94
5	16	10	7 (0.70)	0.95
6	12	4	4 (1.00)	1.00
total	75	29	**20 (0.69)**	0.95

Future work includes a user study in which users are recorded as they walk around the city describing their environment in real-time (rather than describing a route after having walked it). We also plan to analyse in detail whether the individual preference models all have something in common (i.e. whether there are general properties of salience models that always hold). The results of such an analysis might allow us to restrict our candidate sets, thereby making it possible to build the models from more examples. Furthermore, we aim to investigate which other features, apart from the ones we are considering in this article, are important for the salience computation problem.

References

1. Boye, J., Fredriksson, M., Götze, J., Gustafson, J. and Königsmann, J. (2012) Walk this way: Spatial grounding for city exploration. *Proc. 4th IWSDS*
2. Denis, M., Pazzaglia, F., Cornoldi, C. and Bertolo, L. (1999) Spatial discourse and navigation: an analysis of route directions in the city of Venice. *Applied cognitive psychology*, vol 13, no 2.
3. Duckham, M., Winter, S. and Robinson, M. (2010) Including landmarks in routing instructions. *Journal of Location Based Services*, vol. 4, no. 1, pp. 28–52.
4. Fiechter, C-N. and Rogers, S. (2000) Learning subjective functions with large margins. *Proc. 17th ICML*, pp. 287–294.
5. Haklay, M. (2008) OpenStreetMap: User-generated street maps. *Pervasive computing IEEE*, vol. 7, issue 4, pp. 12–18.
6. Nothegger, C., Winter, S. and Raubal, M. (2004) Selection of salient features for route directions. *Spatial cognition and computation*, 4(2), pp. 113–136.
7. Papadimitrou, C. and Steiglitz, K. (1982) *Combinatorial optimization: Algorithms and complexity*, Prentice-Hall.
8. Sorrows, M.E. and Hirtle, S.C. (1999). The nature of landmarks for real and electronic spaces. *Spatial information theory: Cognitive and computational foundations of geographic information science*, vol. 1661 LNCS, pp. 37–50.
9. Xia, J., Richter, K-F., Winter, S. and Arnold, L. (2011) A survey to understand the role of landmarks for GPS navigation. *Proc. PATREC research forum.*

Human Evaluation of Conceptual Route Graphs for Interpreting Spoken Route Descriptions

Raveesh Meena, Gabriel Skantze and Joakim Gustafson

Department of Speech, Music and Hearing, KTH, Stockholm, Sweden
raveesh@csc.kth.se, {gabriel, jocke}@speech.kth.se

Abstract. We present a human evaluation of the usefulness of conceptual route graphs (CRGs) when it comes to route following using spoken route descriptions. We describe a method for data-driven semantic interpretation of route descriptions into CRGs. The comparable performances of human participants in sketching a route using the manually transcribed CRGs and the CRGs produced on speech recognized route descriptions indicate the robustness of our method in preserving the vital conceptual information required for route following despite speech recognition errors.

1 Introduction

It is desirable to endow urban robots with capabilities for engaging in spoken dialogue with passersby to seek route directions for autonomous navigation in unknown environments. Understanding spoken route descriptions mandates a robot's dialogue system to have a spoken language understanding (SLU) component that (i) is *robust* in handling automatic speech recognition (ASR) errors, (ii) learns *generalization* to deal with unseen concepts in free speech, and (iii) preserve the highly *structured relations* among various spatial and linguistic concepts present in route descriptions.

A SLU component in a dialogue system takes an ASR hypothesis as input and outputs a semantic representation that can be used by the dialogue manager to decide the next course of actions. A common way of representing navigational knowledge is the *route graph*. While varying level of details could be specified in a route graph (e.g. metric route graph), they are not representative of how humans structure information in route descriptions. Thus, a *conceptual route graph* (CRG) [1], is needed that can be used to represent human route descriptions semantically. In [2], we have presented a novel approach for data-driven semantic interpretation of manually transcribed route descriptions into CRGs. More recently, in [3] we applied this approach for semantic interpretation of spoken route descriptions. The results indicate that our approach is robust in handling ASR errors. The question as to whether the generated CRGs could actually be used by an agent in following the described route and arrive at the intended destination was left as future work.

In this paper, we evaluate the usefulness of the automatically extracted CRGs by asking human participants to sketch the described route on a map. Such an objective evaluation offers an alternative approach to evaluate our method: comparable human performances using the manually transcribed CRGs and the CRGs produced from speech recognized results would confirm the robustness of our method in preserving vital conceptual information for route following, despite speech recognition errors. In addition, a detailed analysis of human performances would help us (i) identify areas for further improvement in our method and the model, and also (ii) assess the usefulness of CRGs as a semantic representation for freely spoken route descriptions.

2 Previous work

It has been established in the literature that route descriptions contain a lot of redundant information whereas only a limited set of details are actually necessary for route following. These include descriptions about: the *landmarks* on the route, the *spatial relations*, the *controllers* that ensure traversal along the intended route, and the *actions* for changing orientation. Both data-driven and grammar based parsing approaches for semantic interpretation of route descriptions have been presented and evaluated for route following through human participants and/or robots in real and/or virtual environments [4-8]. Most of these works have focused on interpreting manually transcribed or human written route descriptions. Understanding verbal route descriptions has not received much attention. In [4] an ASR system has been used for recognizing verbal route descriptions, but the recognized text was translated to primitive routines using a translation scheme. In the following section, we briefly describe our data-driven approach for semantic interpretation of spoken route descriptions into CRGs, which have been shown to be useful in robot navigation [5].

2.1 A chunking parser for semantic interpretation

Our approach in [2] is a novel application of Abney's *chunking parser* [9], in which we apply the *Chunker* and the *Attacher* stages to automatically extract CRGs from route descriptions. A CRG is similar to a route graph in that nodes represent places where a change in direction takes place and edges connect these places. A route graph (or a *route*) may be divided into route *segments*, where each segment consists of an edge and an ending node where an action to change direction takes place. Conceptually, a segment consists of (i) *controllers* – a set of descriptions that guide the traversal along the edge, e.g. "*go straight down that road*", (ii) *routers* – a set of place descriptors that helps to identify the ending node, e.g. "*turn left at the post-office*", and (iii) *action* – the action to take at the ending node in order to change direction. At least one of these three components is required in a route segment.

Fig. 1 illustrates an example CRG in which the nodes represent the semantic concepts and the edges their attributes. The concepts, their attributes and argument types are defined in the type hierarchy of the domain model using the specification in the JINDIGO dialogue framework [10].

To automatically extract CRGs, we first apply the *Chunker* stage of the Chunking parser for finding *base* concepts in a given sequence of words. Another chunk learner, namely the *Segmenter*, is then applied to automatically learn *route segments* in a sequence of base concepts. The *Attacher* takes a route segment as input and performs two tasks for each base concept present in it: First, it may assign a more specific concept class (like POSTOFFICE). To allow it to generalize, the Attacher also assigns all ancestor classes, based on the domain model (i.e. BUILDING for POSTOFFICE). The second task for the Attacher is to assign attributes, e.g. *direction,* and assign them values, e.g. →, which means that the interpreter should look for a matching argument in the right context. Table 1 illustrates these three stages for parsing the route description "*turn left at eh the post-office and then take...*"

Table 1. The three stages of the Chunking parser for interpreting route descriptions.

Chunker	[**ACTION** *turn*] [**DIRECTION** *left*] [**ROUTER** *at*] [**FP** *eh*] [**LANDMARK** *the post-office*] [**SCONT** *and then*] [**ACTION** *take*]
Segmenter	[**SEGMENT** [ACTION *turn*] [DIRECTION *left*] [ROUTER *at*] [FP *eh*] [LANDMARK *the post-office*]] [**SEGMENT** [SCONT *and then*] [ACTION *take*]]
Attacher	[SEGMENT [**TURN** (*direction*: →) *turn*] [**LEFT** *left*] [**AT** (*landmark*: →) *at*] [**DM** *eh*] [**POSTOFFICE** *the post-office*]] [SEGMENT [**DM** *and then*] [**TAKE** *take*]]

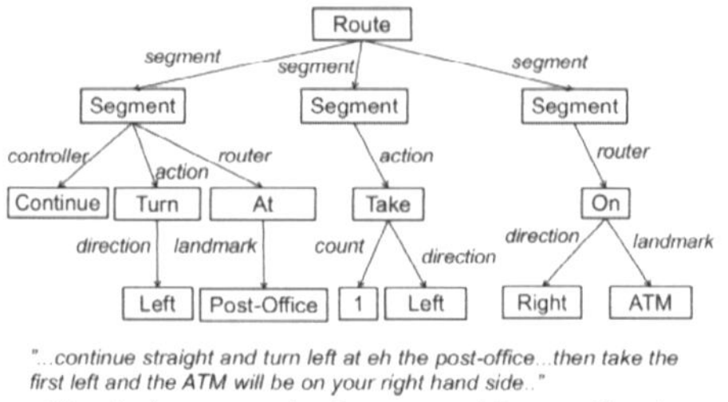

Fig. 1. An example Conceptual Route Graph.

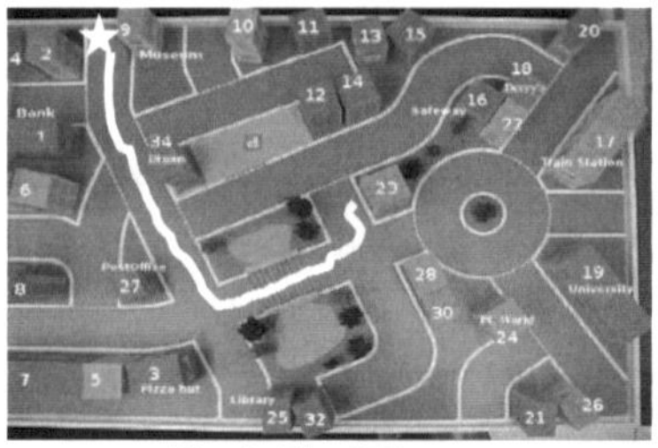
Fig. 2. The IBL map.

To measure the performance of our method we used the notion of Concept Error Rate (CER) – the weighted sum of the edits required in the manually transcribed CRG to obtain the extracted CRG. To evaluate our method we used the IBL corpora, which contain audio recordings and manual transcriptions of 144 spoken route instructions given in English [11]. Thirty five IBL transcriptions were manually annotated and used as the cross-validation set. Using the Linear Threshold Unit algorithms and best feature combinations discussed in [3], a baseline CER of 18.04 was obtained for comparing the Chunking parser's performance on speech recognized results.

Next, we trained an off-the-shelf ASR system with the remaining 108 route descriptions. For the best speech recognized hypothesis (mean WER = 27.59) for the route descriptions in the cross-validation set we obtained a CER of 28.15, i.e., a relative increase of mere 10.11 in CER. The relative increase in CER (R-CER) remains rather steady (SD = 2.80) with increase in WER. This illustrates the robustness of our method in dealing with speech recognition errors.

3 Method

Material: Six IBL route descriptions from the set of 35 were used for human evaluation. Care was taken in selecting routes to ensure that subjects could not guess the destination. For each route we obtained four instruction types: (1) the IBL manual transcription (ManTsc), (2) the manually annotated CRG (crgMAN), (3) the CRG extracted from the IBL manual transcription (crgCMT), and (4) the CRG extracted from the speech recognized route description (crgASR). The 24 items resulting from this combination were rearranged into four sets, each comprising of the six routes, but differing in the instruction type for the routes.

Subjects: A total of 16 humans (13 male and 3 female) participated in the evaluation. Participants ranged in the age from 16 to 46 (mean = 30.87, *SD* = 7.74). All, but one were researchers or graduate students in computer science.

Procedure: Participants were asked to sketch the route, on the IBL map (cf. Fig. 2, the star indicates the starting place), corresponding to the provided instruction. Each participant was individually introduced to the basic concept types in CRGs and shown how a route could be planned using the various nodes and sub-graphs in a CRG. Participants were asked to also mark concepts that they thought were absolutely necessary and strike-out what was redundant for the task at hand. Each of the four sets was evaluated by four different participants.

3.1 Results and analysis

We classified the 96 human performances under three categories: (1) FOUND: the participant arrived at the target building following the intended path, (2) ALM_THERE: the participant has almost arrived at the target building following the intended path, but did not correctly identify it among the others, (3) NOT_FOUND: the participant lost her way and did not arrive at the target building. Fig. 3 provides an overview of these performances across the four instruction types. One-way ANOVA test indicates a significant difference between only the human performances across crgASR and ManTsc instructions ($p < 0.05$). This is not surprising given that the crgASR instructions were produced from speech recognized results with WER of 47.64 (*SD* = 7.98) and have a R-CER of 27.35. However, there is no significant difference in performances across the crgMAN, crgCMT and crgASR instructions. This suggests that the conceptual information, required for human route following, present in Chunker parser produced CRGs is comparable with the information present in manually annotated CRGs, despite the CER of 20.29 and R-CER of 27.35 for crgCMT and crgASR instructions respectively.

These results confirm the robust performance of Chunking parser in dealing with speech recognition errors and preserving the vital conceptual information. Moreover, the results also suggest that improving the model (i.e. the CRG representation) to reduce the gap between human performances for ManTsc and crgMAN instructions will further enhance the human performances for Chunking parser extracted CRGs.

A closer analysis of the ALM_THERE (13) and NOT_FOUND (20) performances (a total of 33) suggest five general problem categories: (1) *SpatialR*: spatial relations, (2) *Controller*, (3) *Action*, (4) *Landmark*, and (5) *Other*: human errors. Across these five problem categories five sources were identified: (1) *Annotation*: an incorrect or underspecified manual annotation, (2) *ASR*: concepts insertion or deletion during speech recognition, (3) *ChunkingP*: Chunking parser errors, (4) *Model*: a limitation of the current model, and (5) *Human*: human judgments about the relevance or redundancy of a concept and executing actions.

The distribution of these error sources across the problem categories, as illustrated in Fig. 4, indicates that majority of the problems pertain to spatial relations (51.51%) and *Controllers* (24.24%). While some of the problems with the spatial relations are a result of incorrect and underspecified annotations (9.09%), which may have contributed to Chunking parser errors (9.09%) and to an extent to human judgments (21.21%), manual observations suggest that the overall human performance could have been better with the inclusion of additional spatial relation and *Controller* types in the model. We have refrained from elaborate annotations in the current model due to limited amount of training data. Human judgments were the source of half of the errors (51.51%). This indicates that it wasn't always easy to make the right decision about discarding or using concepts in the CRGs for route planning.

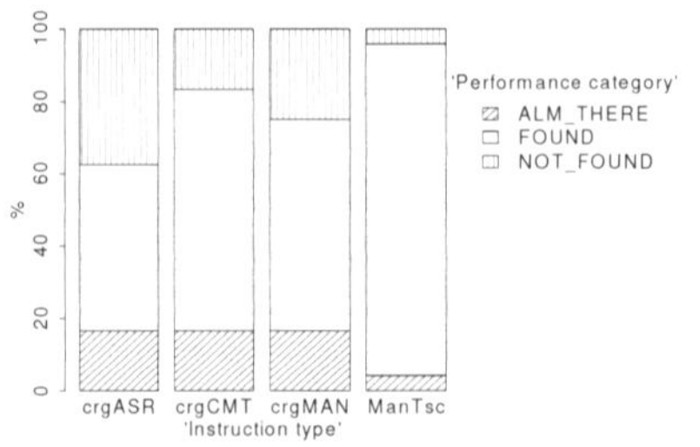

Fig. 3. Human performances across the instructions types.

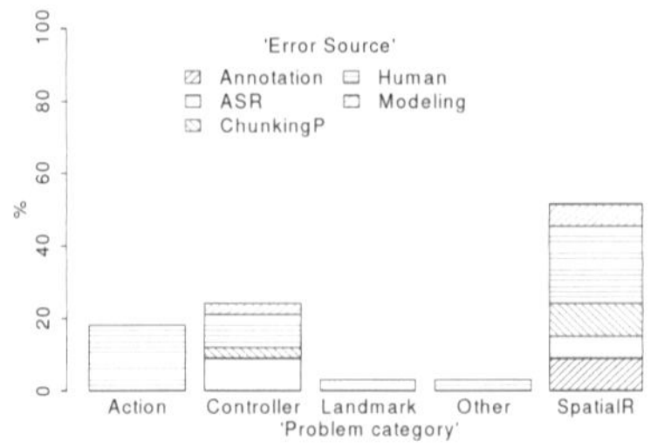

Fig. 4. Distribution of error sources across the problem categories.

4 Discussion and conclusion

From this human evaluation exercise we note that:

- *Controllers* with travel distance argument are vital for representing the extent of movement in a particular direction in route descriptions, such as "*follow the road to its end on the right is the treasure*" or "*a few buildings down from Pizza-Hut*".
- A requisite for proper grounding of the spatial relations in CRGs is resolving their *direction* or *landmark* arguments, or even both. The *Attacher's* role in attaching the concept RIGHT in CRG "[BUILDING *Tescos*] [AT (*landmark*: ←) *is on*] [RIGHT *right*]", as the *direction* argument for spatial relation AT is essential for locating the landmark.
- The CRG representations for spoken route description contain redundant concepts that arise from speech phenomena, such as pronominal references, anaphoric descriptions, self-repair and repetitions, about *landmarks* and *actions*. The CRG representation for "*you will take the third exit off...the third exit will be for Plymouth university...take this third exit*", contains two *actions* and four *landmarks*. Grounding this to a simple "*take the third exit*" would require additional approaches.
- ASR errors pose another challenge for an agent in route planning using the CRGs. Without access to the topological view of the environment a robot could not possibly infer erroneous concept insertions. To deal with this, we believe clarification or

reprise of route segments would be a prudent strategy, provided that the clarification sub-dialogue itself doesn't lead to further errors.

We have presented a human evaluation of the usefulness of conceptual route graphs – extracted from spoken route descriptions using our data-driven method – for route following. The comparable human performances on sketching the route using the manually transcribed and automatically extracted CRGs suggest no significant loss of conceptual information, required for route following, during the semantic interpretation of verbal route descriptions. This illustrates the robustness of our method in preserving vital conceptual information despite ASR errors. We observe that, extracting CRGs from spoken route descriptions mandates integration of approaches to counter speech phenomena, such as anaphoric descriptions and self-repairs, and using clarification strategies to recover from erroneous concept insertions during ASR.

Acknowledgement

This research was funded by the Swedish research council (VR) project "Incremental processing in multimodal conversational systems" (#2011-6237) and the European Commission project IURO, (#248314).

References

1. Müller, R., Röfer, T., Lankenau, A., Musto, A., Stein, K., & Eisenkolb, A. (2000). Coarse qualitative descriptions in robot navigation. In Freksa, C., Brauer, W., Habel, C., & Wender, K-F. (Eds.), *Spatial Cognition II* (pp. 265-276). Springer.
2. Johansson, M., Skantze, G., & Gustafson, J. (2011). Understanding route directions in human-robot dialogue. In *Proc. of SemDial* (pp. 19-27). Los Angeles, CA.
3. Meena, R., Skantze, G., & Gustafson, J. (2012). A Data-driven Approach to Understanding Spoken Route Directions in Human-Robot Dialogue. *Interspeech*. Portland, OR.
4. Bugmann, G., Klein, E., Lauria, S., & Kyriacou, T. (2004). Corpus-Based Robotics: A Route Instruction Example. In Groen, F. (Ed.), *IAS, vol. 8* (pp. 96-103).
5. Mandel, C., Frese, U., & Rofer, T. (2006). Robot navigation based on the mapping of coarse qualitative route descriptions to route graphs. In *Proc. of IEEE/RSJ IRS* (pp. 205-210). Beijing, China.
6. Kollar, T., Tellex, S., Roy, D., & Roy, N. (2010). Toward understanding natural language directions. In *Proc. of 5th ACM/IEEE HRI* (pp. 259-266). Piscataway, NJ, US. IEEE Press.
7. Pappu, A., & Rudnicky, A. I. (2012). The Structure and Generality of Spoken Route Instructions. In *Proc. of SIGDIAL* (pp. 99-107). Seoul, South Korea. ACL.
8. MacMahon, M., Stankiewicz, B., & Kuipers, B. (2006). Walk the talk: connecting language, knowledge, and action in route instructions. In *Proc. of the 21st national conference on Artificial intelligence - vol. 2* (pp. 1475-1482). AAAI Press.
9. Abney, S. (1991). Parsing by chunks. In Berwick, R. C., Abney, S. P., & Tenny, C. (Eds.), *Principle-Based Parsing: Computation and Psycholinguistics* (pp. 257-278). Kluwer.
10. Skantze, G. (2010). *Jindigo: a Java-based Framework for Incremental Dialogue Systems*. Technical Report, KTH, Stockholm, Sweden.
11. Kyriacou, T., Bugmann, G., & Lauria, S. (2005). Vision-based urban navigation procedures for verbally instructed robots. *Robotics and Autonomous Systems, 51*(1), (pp. 69-80).

Clock-Modeled Ternary Spatial Relations for Visual Scene Analysis

Joanna Isabelle Olszewska

School of Computing and Engineering, University of Huddersfield
Queensgate, Huddersfield, HD1 3DH, United Kingdom
j.olszewska@hud.ac.uk

Abstract. The analysis and the description of complex visual scenes characterized by the presence of many objects of interests involve reasoning on spatial relations such as "above", "below","before", "after" and "between". In this context, we have defined these semantic concepts in terms of ternary spatial relations and we have formalized them using the clock model which is based on the clock-face division and the semantic notions of hours to describe relative spatial positions. The presented approach has been efficiently applied for the automated understanding of spatial relations between multiple objects in real-world computer vision image datasets.

Keywords: Ternary Spatial Relations; Clock Model; Qualitative Spatial Reasoning; Computer Vision; Visual Scene Understanding.

1 Introduction

Modelling spatial relations among objects of visual scenes is greatly of benefit to visual applications [1]. Indeed, their integration into vision systems brings an additional level in the task of automatic image understanding, leading to the processing of semantic information besides those provided by visual features. Furthermore, the definition of spatial relations allows the action of reasoning on semantically meaningful concepts which is a major advantage [3] compared with traditional vision approaches using only quantitative techniques or annotating images with just sparse words.

In the literature, most of the spatial relations [2], [4] have been defined as binary ones, such as the topological spatial relations like the RCC-8 model [5] or the cardinal spatial relations and their fuzzy extension [6].

In context of visual scene description and analysis, [7] introduced a new formalism for modeling the image space as a clock face and they proposed a series of related spatial relations, including the directional spatial relations of the scene objects and the far/close relations. However, to perform reasoning on spatial relations among a greater number of objects (at least three), there is a need for relations such as the ternary ones. In fact, little attention has been paid to study them. Their formal geometric modeling has been mostly studied for geographic information systems (GIS) [8]. Indeed, [9] developed the 5-intersection model, but its formalism leads to a restricted range of applications. On the other hand, [10] proposed for the biomedical imaging purpose a fuzzy definition of the ternary spatial relation *between*. Despite its improvement by [11], it does not fit well for computer vision applications such as crowd's behaviour study.

In this work, we present the extension of the clock approach [7] to formalize the fundamental ternary spatial relation, namely, *between* (bt), and to model the semantic concepts *above* (ab), *below* (bl), $before$ (bf), and $after$ (af) as ternary spatial relations.

We implement these relations using Description Logics (DL) [12] which have been widely adopted for knowledge representation in visual systems [13], [14], [15], [16].

Thus, our clock-modeled ternary spatial relations define a set of useful notions to characterize visual scenes involving numerous objects of interest as well as to acquire knowledge about them, and could be incorporated in a complete system for automatic reasoning on spatial relations among objects detected in images.

The contributions of this paper are as follows:

- the modeling of ternary spatial relations using the clock-face approach;
- the architecture of the full system combining visual face recognition and spatial reasoning.

The paper is structured as follows. In Section 2, we present our approach using the clock formalism to model ternary spatial relations such as *above*, *below*, $before$, $after$, and *between*. All these relations have been integrated in a framework for automatic face recognition and reasoning as described in Section 3. The resulting system has been successfully tested on still image datasets as reported and discussed in Section 4. Conclusions are drawn up in Section 5.

2 Clock-Modeled Ternary Spatial Relations

In Section 2.1, we first introduce the clock model which is semantically meaningful and used to defined spatial relative relations, while the definitions of the ternary spatial relations formalized with this clock model are presented in Section 2.2.

2.1 Clock Model

The clock concept introduced by [7] consists in dividing the image plane in twelve parts around any object of interest of the scene as illustrated in Fig. 1(a). Hence, each portion of the space is then corresponding to an hour. This leads to a semantically meaningful division of the space as a clock face. This concept helps in reducing the uncertainty on the directional relative positions between objects in crowded scenes, in which case traditional binary relations such as $left$ or *right* are not enough discriminant as demonstrated in [7]. In this work, the clock notion is used for the formal specification of our ternary relative directional relations *above*, *below*, $before$, $after$, and *between*.

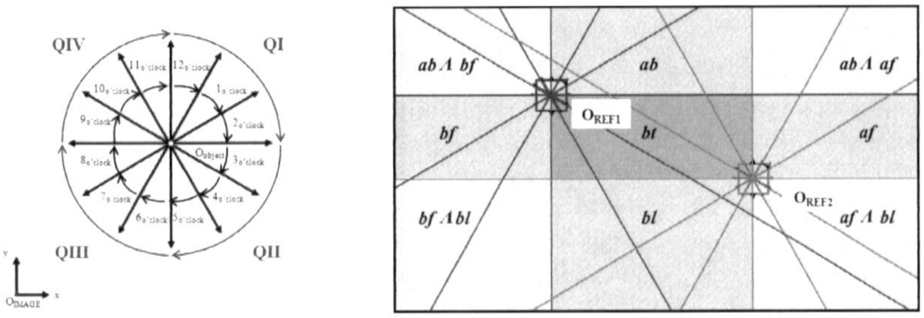

(a) Clock model (b) Clock-modeled ternary spatial relations

Fig. 1. Illustration of the ternary spatial relations between visual objects using the clock model (a) and representing the semantic concepts which are *above* (*ab*), *below* (*bl*), *before* (*bf*), *after* (*af*), and *between* (*bt*) (b).

For this purpose, we introduce the *Quadrant* (Q) concept as shown in Fig. 1(a). To provide an example of how we have formalized it, we define $isInQuadrantIOf$ in DL as follows. Let O_{REF} be the object of reference and the O_{REL} the target object. Giving that *Angle* is the relative angle between the line $O_{REF} - O_{REL}$ and the axis X of the analyzed image plane, then

$$\begin{aligned} isInQuadrantIOf \sqsubseteq\ & Spatial\_Relation \sqcap \exists hasReferentObject.O_{REF} \\ & \sqcap \exists hasTargetObject.O_{REL} \sqcap (\exists hasAngle.Angle12clock \\ & \sqcup \exists hasAngle.Angle1clock \sqcup \exists hasAngle.Angle2clock) \end{aligned} \quad (1)$$

with

$$Angle2clock \equiv Angle \sqcap \exists Angle.value{\leq}\ \frac{\pi}{6} \sqcap \exists Angle.value{>}\ 0 \quad (2)$$

Equation (2) denotes the set of angles which have values lower than or equal to $\pi/6$ and higher than 0. In this example, $value{\leq}\ \frac{\pi}{6}$ is a predicate over the real number domain $\mathbb{R}$. *Angle12clock* and *Angle1clock* concepts are defined similarly. We can note also that any O_{REL} lies at least in one of the four quadrants QI, QII, $QIII$ or QIV.

2.2 Ternary Spatial Relations

We adopt the notation $rl(A, B, C)$ for a ternary relation rl among three objects A, B, and C. The first object A involved in this relation is considered to be the target object, whereas the two other objects B and C are the reference objects. Thus, $rl(A, B, C)$ denotes that "A is in the relation rl with B and C". In fact, the order of the reference objects B and C is important as it affects the orientation of the relation, in this case from the reference object B to the reference object C. While in some relations the role of the three objects can be exchanged without affecting the relation, in some relations the swapping of the arguments leads to a change of the relation.

In the remaining of this section, we present the detailed definitions of the relations *above*, *below*, *before*, and *after* which are formalized in this work as ternary spatial relations in opposite to [10] or [11], as well as the relation *between*, and we mention the cases when the exchange of the arguments modifies the described relations. It is worth to note that the definitions are valid for both convex and concave objects and that the center of each related clock is set to the centroid of the corresponding object.

Spatial Relation *Above* We consider the relation *above* as a ternary spatial relation where $ab(O_{REL}, O_{REF1}, O_{REF2})$ means that the target object O_{REL} is above both the reference object O_{REF1} and the reference object O_{REF2}. For this relation, the order of the reference objects cannot be inverted otherwise the type of the relation is modified. Indeed, if the target object is above only one of the reference objects, other ternary spatial relations can be then applied. Hence, this ternary modeling leads to a more discriminating relation than the traditional ones in particular in the case of crowded scene analysis.

In DL, the concept *isAbove* is defined as follows. Let O_{REF1} and O_{REF2} be the two objects of reference, while O_{REL} is the object of interest. Considering definitions such as expressed by Eqs. (1) and (2), then

$$\begin{aligned} isAbove \sqsubseteq\ & Spatial\_Relation \sqcap Ternary\_Spatial\_Relation \\ & \sqcap \exists hasReferentObject.O_{REF1} \sqcap \exists hasReferentObject.O_{REF2} \\ & \sqcap \exists hasTargetObject.O_{REL} \sqcap (\exists isInQuadrantIVOf.O_{REF1} \\ & \sqcup \exists isInQuadrantIOf.O_{REF1}) \sqcap (\exists isInQuadrantIVOf.O_{REF2} \\ & \sqcup \exists isInQuadrantIOf.O_{REF2}). \end{aligned} \tag{3}$$

This concept is illustrated in Fig. 1(b).

Spatial Relation *Below* We consider the relation *below* as a ternary spatial relation where $bl(O_{REL}, O_{REF1}, O_{REF2})$ means that the target object O_{REL} is below both the reference object O_{REF1} and the reference object O_{REF2}. For this relation, the order of the reference objects cannot be inverted otherwise the type of the relation is modified. Indeed, if the target object is below only one of the reference objects, other ternary spatial relations can be then applied. Hence, this ternary modeling leads to a more discriminating relation than the traditional ones in particular in the case of crowded scene analysis.

In DL, the concept *isBelow* is defined as follows. Let O_{REF1} and O_{REF2} be the two objects of reference, while O_{REL} is the object of interest. Considering definitions such as expressed by Eqs. (1) and (2), then

$$\begin{aligned} isBelow \sqsubseteq\ & Spatial\_Relation \sqcap Ternary\_Spatial\_Relation \\ & \sqcap \exists hasReferentObject.O_{REF1} \sqcap \exists hasReferentObject.O_{REF2} \\ & \sqcap \exists hasTargetObject.O_{REL} \sqcap (\exists isInQuadrantIIOf.O_{REF1} \\ & \sqcup \exists isInQuadrantIIIOf.O_{REF1}) \sqcap (\exists isInQuadrantIIOf.O_{REF2} \\ & \sqcup \exists isInQuadrantIIIOf.O_{REF2}). \end{aligned} \tag{4}$$

A representation of this concept is depicted in Fig. 1(b).

Spatial Relation *Before* We consider the relation *before* as a ternary spatial relation where $bf(O_{REL}, O_{REF1}, O_{REF2})$ means that the target object O_{REL} is before both the reference object O_{REF1} and the reference object O_{REF2}. For this relation, the order of the reference objects cannot be inverted otherwise the type of the relation is modified. Indeed, if the target object is before only one of the reference objects, other ternary spatial relations can be then applied. Hence, this ternary modeling leads to a more discriminating relation than the traditional ones in particular in the case of crowded scene analysis.

In DL, the concept *isBefore* is defined as follows. Let O_{REF1} and O_{REF2} be the two objects of reference, while O_{REL} is the object of interest. Considering definitions such as expressed by Eqs. (1) and (2), then

$$\begin{aligned} isBefore \sqsubseteq\ & Spatial\_Relation \sqcap Ternary\_Spatial\_Relation \\ & \sqcap \exists hasReferentObject.O_{REF1} \sqcap \exists hasReferentObject.O_{REF2} \\ & \sqcap \exists hasTargetObject.O_{REL} \sqcap (\exists isInQuadrantIIIOf.O_{REF1} \\ & \sqcup \exists isInQuadrantIVOf.O_{REF1}) \sqcap (\exists isInQuadrantIIIOf.O_{REF2} \\ & \sqcup \exists isInQuadrantIVOf.O_{REF2}). \end{aligned} \tag{5}$$

An illustration of this concept is depicted in Fig. 1(b).

Spatial Relation *After* We consider the relation *after* as a ternary spatial relation where $af(O_{REL}, O_{REF1}, O_{REF2})$ means that the target object O_{REL} is after both the reference object O_{REF1} and the reference object O_{REF2}. For this relation, the order of the reference objects cannot be inverted otherwise the type of the relation is modified. Indeed, if the target object is after only one of the reference objects, other ternary spatial relations can be then applied. Hence, this ternary modeling leads to a more discriminating relation than the traditional ones in particular in the case of crowded scene analysis.

In DL, the concept *isAfter* is defined as follows. Let O_{REF1} and O_{REF2} be the two objects of reference, while O_{REL} is the object of interest. Considering definitions such as expressed by Eqs. (1) and (2), then

$$\begin{aligned} isBefore \sqsubseteq\ & Spatial\_Relation \sqcap Ternary\_Spatial\_Relation \\ & \sqcap \exists hasReferentObject.O_{REF1} \sqcap \exists hasReferentObject.O_{REF2} \\ & \sqcap \exists hasTargetObject.O_{REL} \sqcap (\exists isInQuadrantIOf.O_{REF1} \\ & \sqcup \exists isInQuadrantIIOf.O_{REF1}) \sqcap (\exists isInQuadrantIOf.O_{REF2} \\ & \sqcup \exists isInQuadrantIIOf.O_{REF2}). \end{aligned} \tag{6}$$

This concept could be visualized in Fig. 1(b).

Spatial Relation *Between* The relation *between* is intrinsically a ternary spatial relation. Indeed, $bt(O_{REL}, O_{REF1}, O_{REF2})$ means that the target object O_{REL} is between the reference object O_{REF1} and the reference object O_{REF2}. In this case, the order of the reference objects can be inverted without changing the semantic meaning of this relation.

In DL, the concept $isBetween$ is defined as follows. Considering definitions such as expressed by Eqs. (3)-(6), then

$$\begin{aligned} isBetween \sqsubseteq\ & Spatial\_Relation \sqcap Ternary\_Spatial\_Relation \\ & \sqcap \exists inverse.isAbove \sqcap \exists inverse.isBelow \\ & \sqcap \exists inverse.isBefore \sqcap \exists inverse.isAfter. \end{aligned} \tag{7}$$

This concept is illustrated in Fig. 1(b).

3 Implementation

The ternary spatial relations described in Section 2 could be embedded into a system for the automatic analysis of people localization in imaged scenes as presented in Fig. 2. Indeed, understanding images with groups of people is a complex process which requires more information that just those contained in the extracted visual features. In [17], they propose to add social relations in order to improve the automatic analysis of this kind of images, but their estimations are less satisfactory compared to those we obtain (see Section 4) by adding the presented spatial relations to the vision system.

The developed system is composed of three main phases. The first two steps constitute a vision system for face detection, which has been implemented using the well-established method of [18]. Firstly, faces are learned by training the system on sets of positive and negative examples, respectively. Secondly, the resulting face detector is applied on an image and automatically computes faces' locations which are then included in corresponding rectangles and labeled. Then, the quantitative data which are extracted by this process are transferred in a similar way to [19] or [14] in order to populate an ontology such as [13]. This ontology is enhanced with the proposed ternary spatial relations. Next, qualitative reasoning is performed on these spatial relations and FaCT++ is used as the reasoner. This last phase of the system thus consists in reasoning on the ternary spatial relations and has been assessed in Section 4.

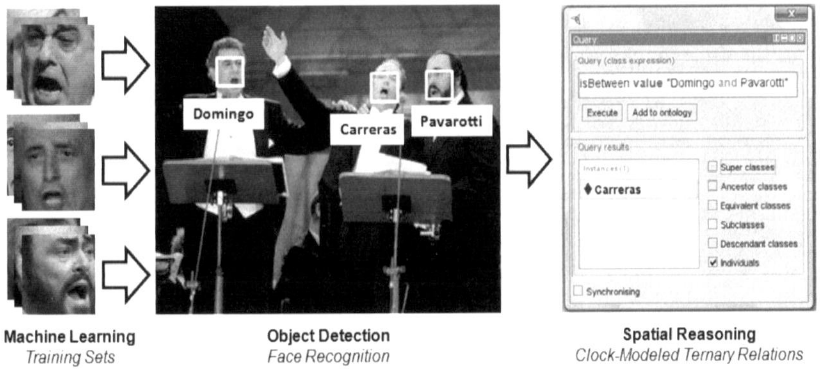

Fig. 2. Overview of our proposed system for reasoning on ternary spatial relations between detected visual objects to automatically understand scenes.

4 Experiments and Discussion

The goals of the presented experiments are twofold. On one hand, we assess in a quantitative way the performance of the all five proposed ternary relations compared to the 5-intersection model which is the only one also defining *above*, *below*, *before*, *after* as ternary relations, but using a different formalism from ours. On the other hand, qualitative assessment of our relations is performed against the ground truth.

In order to evaluate the performance of our formalism of all the ternary proposed relations, our relations have been embedded in the overall system developed for the computer vision application consisting in the analysis of photos with groups of people such as presented in Fig. 2.

To carry out these tests, we have firstly retrieved from Internet images of choirs using Google Image. The aim of the search of choir images was to ensure the finding of pictures of groups of people to analyze spatial relations among them. Indeed, the direct keywords "groups of people" did not produce relevant results. Then, we have constituted a dataset with these 500 retrieved choirs images where faces have been detected and labeled as explained in Section 3. The picture of Fig. 3(a) is an example of the images composing the dataset. Although the study of the face detection problem is out of purpose of the present paper, we can mention that the obtained general precision rate was 95% and that the undetected faces were manually added for the completeness of the dataset.

The adopted criterion for the quantitative assessment of a ternary spatial relation $rl(A, B, C)$ is the satisfaction degree computed as follows

$$s(A) = \frac{|area(A) \cap \Gamma_{BC}|}{|area(A)|}, \tag{8}$$

where A is the target object and Γ_{BC} is the area between the two reference objects B and C.

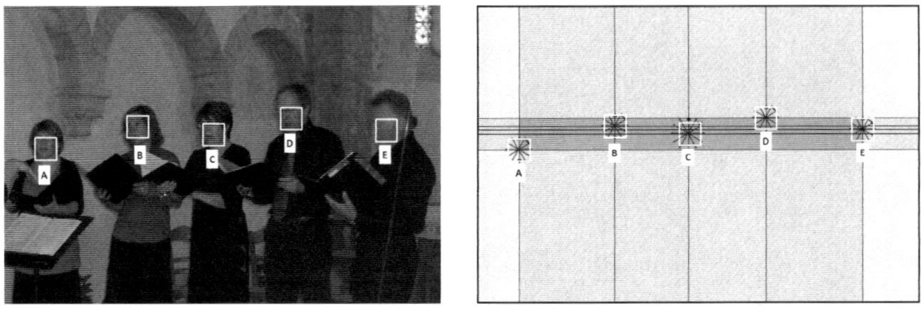

(a) (b)

Fig. 3. Results of our system tested for an image of a choir. First column: Face recognition results. Second column: Schematic spatial representation of the *above*, *below*, *before*, *after*, and *between* relations of the visual objects detected in the image under study.

The qualitative evaluation of the system is carried out by asking different questions whose answers are boolean. The two main types of possible queries are:

- what are the relation(s) among three given objects O_{REL}, O_{REF1}, and O_{REF2}?
- which is/are the object(s) O_{REL} that have the relation rl with the given objects O_{REF1}, and O_{REF2}?

In the case of the image of the Fig. 3(a), the quantitative and qualitative results are reported in Tables 1 and 2, respectively.

When compared with the ternary relations of [9], we assume the semantic correspondence between their *leftside* concept and our *above* concept as well as between their *rightside* concept and our *below* concept.

Table 1. Quantitative evaluation of the ternary relations for the objects in the choir image in Fig. 3(a).

			Approaches									
			from [9]					ours (Sec. 2)				
O_{REL}	O_{REF1}	O_{REF2}	ab	bl	bf	af	bt	ab	bl	bf	af	bt
B	A	D	0.48	0.00	0.00	0.00	0.52	0.18	0.00	0.00	0.00	0.82
C	A	B	0.00	0.43	0.00	0.57	0.00	0.18	0.00	0.00	1.00	0.00
C	A	D	0.00	0.20	0.00	0.00	0.80	0.00	0.00	0.00	0.00	1.00
C	D	E	0.00	0.00	0.50	0.00	0.50	0.00	0.68	1.00	0.00	0.00
D	A	C	0.07	0.00	0.00	0.93	0.00	1.00	0.00	0.00	1.00	0.00

Table 2. Qualitative evaluation of the ternary relations for the objects in the choir image in Fig. 3(a).

			Approaches									
			ground truth					ours (Sec. 2)				
O_{REL}	O_{REF1}	O_{REF2}	*ab*	*bl*	*bf*	*af*	*bt*	*ab*	*bl*	*bf*	*af*	*bt*
A	*C*	*E*	no	yes	yes	no	no	no	yes	yes	no	no
B	*A*	*C*	yes	no	no	no	yes	yes	no	no	no	yes
B	*C*	*D*	no	no	yes	no	no	no	no	yes	no	no
C	*B*	*D*	no	yes	no	no	yes	no	yes	no	no	yes
D	*A*	*B*	yes	no	no	yes	no	yes	no	no	yes	no
E	*A*	*B*	no	no	no	yes	no	no	no	no	yes	no

In Table 1, we can observe that in the case of the relation $rl(C, A, D)$, we find that the object C is between A and D when applying our formalism, whereas [9] considers that the object C is also below the objects A and D that is not complying with the human intuition. For the relations such as $rl(B, A, D)$ or $rl(C, D, E)$, our approach provides values which indicate the dominant relation between these objects and which is each time conformed with the human perception of the scene. In opposite, the figures computed using [9] give a large uncertainty about the type of the relations among the objects, e.g. by finding (i) 50% for C below D and E and (ii) 50% for C between D and E which does not indicate which semantic relation is correct and makes confusion between true (ii) and false (i) statements.

In the results of the qualitative reasoning on the proposed ternary spatial relations as reported in Table 2, we note the excellent concordance between the ground truth values set by human users and those computed with our developed system. The overall precision of our system tested for the entire dataset is of 99.5 ± 0.5 %.

Hence, the evaluation of the results shows that our clock-based formalism provides a more accurate and consistent definition of these concepts than the state-of-the art ones.

5 Conclusions

In this paper, we have applied new ternary spatial relations, namely, *above*, *below*, *before*, *after*, and *between*, in order to automatically understand and interpret images with complex content such as groups of people. Formalizing the presented relations using the clock model and defining them as ternary relations has provided new powerful semantic concepts to describe the relative position of an object of interest towards two other distinct visual objects. As demonstrated, this conceptualization brings a new insight in the automated analysis of crowded visual scenes.

References

1. Dobnik S.: Coordinating Spatial Perspective in Discourse. In: Proceedings of the EPSRC Workshop on Vision and Language, Sheffield, UK (2012)
2. Dimanzo M., Adorni G., Giunchiglia F.: Reasoning about Scene Descriptions. Proceedings of IEEE. 74, 1013–1025 (1986)
3. Cohn A. G., Renz J.: Qualitative Spatial Reasoning. In: Handbook of Knowledge Representation. Elsevier (2007)
4. Ligozat G.: Qualitative Spatial and Temporal Reasoning. John Wiley & Sons (2011)
5. Randell D. A., Cui Z., Cohn A. G.: A Spatial Logic Based on Regions and Connection. In: Proceedings of the International Conference on Knowledge Representation and Reasoning, pp. 165–176 (1992)
6. Hudelot C., Atif J., Bloch I.: Fuzzy Spatial Relation Ontology for Image Interpretation. Fuzzy Sets and Systems. 159, 1929–1951 (2008)
7. Olszewska J. I., McCluskey T. L.: Ontology-Coupled Active Contours for Dynamic Video Scene Understanding. In: Proceedings of the IEEE International Conference on Intelligent Engineering Systems, pp. 369–374 (2011)
8. Clementini E., Skiadopoulos S., Billen R., Tarquini F.: A Reasoning System of Ternary Projective Relations. IEEE Transactions on Knowledge and Data Engineering. 22, 161–178 (2010)
9. Clementini E., Billen R.: Modeling and Computing Ternary Projective Relations Between Regions. IEEE Transactions on Knowledge and Data Engineering. 18, 799–814 (2006)
10. Bloch I., Colliot O., Cesar Jr, R. M.: On the Ternary Spatial Relation "Between". IEEE Transactions on Systems, Man, and Cybernetics - Part B: Cybernetics. 36, 312–327 (2006)
11. Gokberk Cinbis R., Aksoy S.: Relative Position-Based Spatial Relationships Using Mathematical Morphology. In: Proceedings of the IEEE International Conference on Image Processing, pp. II.97–II.100 (2007)
12. Baader F., Calvanese D., McGuinness D. L., Nardi D., Patel-Schneider P. F.: The Description Logic Handbook: Theory, Implementation and Applications. Cambridge University Press, 2nd Ed. (2010)
13. Olszewska J. I.: Spatio-Temporal Visual Ontology. In: Proceedings of the EPSRC Workshop on Vision and Language, Brighton, UK (2011)
14. Olszewska J. I.: Multi-Target Parametric Active Contours to Support Ontological Domain Representation. In: Proceedings of RFIA, pp. 779–784 (2012)
15. Le Ber F., Napoli A.: Object-Based Representation and Classification of Spatial Structures and Relations. In: Proceedings of the IEEE International Conference on Tools with Artificial Intelligence, pp. 268–275 (2002)
16. Neumann B., Moeller R.: On Scene Interpretation with Description Logics. Image and Vision Computing. 26, 114–126 (2008)
17. Gallagher A. C., Chen T.: Understanding Images of Groups of People. In: Proceedings of the IEEE International Conference on Computer Vision and Pattern Recognition, pp. 256–263 (2009)
18. Viola P., Jones M. J.: Robust Real-Time Face Detection. International Journal of Computer Vision, 57, 137–154 (2004)
19. Kohler C., Ottlik A., Nagel H.-H., Nebel B.: Qualitative Reasoning Feeding Back Into Quantitative Model-Based Tracking. In: Proceedings of the European Conference on Artificial Intelligence, pp. 1041–1042 (2004)

Where Things Happen: On the Semantics of Event Localization

James Pustejovsky

Computer Science Department
Brandeis University
Waltham, MA USA

Abstract. The problem of temporally situating events in language has been approached by a number of philosophical techniques, including Davidson's particularist theory of event individuation [6, 5] and Kim's property exemplification theory [16]. Both of these theories have been developed within linguistic semantic traditions, as well (cf. [24, 2] and others). However, the problem of event localization (spatially situating events) has not been discussed as extensively in the semantics literature. In this paper, I discuss the procedures for identifying where events, as expressed in natural language, are located in space. Aspects of the semantics of event localization have been recently proposed, including the notion of the "shape" of a movement [8, 39], as well as treating movement verbs as "path creation" predicates [29]. In this paper, I build on these and some additional observations to outline a more general semantics of event localization. I then outline a procedure that extends the path metaphor used for motion predicates, distinguishing between the event locus and the spatial aspect of an event. In the process, I discuss how localization is supervenient upon the participants in the events.

Keywords: Spatial Language, Event semantics, Qualitative spatial reasoning

1 Introduction

This paper discusses an issue of some importance to both qualitative spatial reasoning (QSR) as well as natural language semantics. The aim of this brief note is to discuss procedures for identifying where events, as expressed in natural language, are located in space. While much fundamental work has been done on modeling the topological and orientatational relations between objects viewed as regions ([30, 3, 7, 1]), the theoretical foundations for a similar calculus of relations for locating eventualities is less developed. Similarly, in linguistic semantics research, the question of where events are spatially located has also been generally neglected, when compared to the effort devoted to the temporal and aspectual interpretation of eventualities. Some notable exceptions to this involve the analysis of motion events, where identification of the path is an inherent aspect of the semantics of the predicate and associated composition with spatial prepositional phrases ([8, 38, 23, 39, 29]).

This paper presents some of the issues pertaining to the semantics of event localization. For the purpose of this paper, *event localization* will refer to the process of identifying the spatial extent of an event, activity, or situation, what we refer to as its *minimum embedding space*. The focus here will be on the interpretation of natural language descriptions of events, and not on event recognition and classification from other modalities, such as sensor arrays or visual input. We argue that the localization of an event appears to depend on three major semantic factors: (i) the internal structure of the event; (ii) its semantic type; and (iii) the specific role that the event participants play in the event. Localization can be defined as the computation of the minimum embedding space, the *event locus*, for the participants in an event. This is the minimum bounding region within which the event transpires, including all relevant participants. Within this space, it is often the case that a relative location is linguistically singled out, what we call the *spatial aspect* of the event. As we demonstrate, when this happens, a semantic distinction is introduced between the locus (figure) and its aspect (ground). We outline the localization procedure for both motion and some non-motion predicates in language, somewhat informally, due to space limitations.

2 Previous Work on Locating Events

To begin, consider the distinction typically made in linguistics in how time and space are interpreted semantically. In earlier philosophical discussions, it was widely assumed (e.g., Vendler [37]) that events are interpreted relative to times, while objects are interpreted relative to locations. For example, the eventualities in (1) can each be temporally situated, giving rise to distinct interpretations in tense, aspect, or genericity.

(1) a. Maria *left* for Warsaw.
b. Piotr *finished* his book.
c. Fred *was eating* a sandwich.
d. Barbara *had invited* me before Eva *wrote* me.
e. Americans *like* pizza and beer.
f. Dinosaurs *roamed* the earth.

Vendler distinguishes such temporal localizations for events from object localizations. Consider the sentences in (2), where the objects participate in an inherent spatial relation, which can be temporally anchored.

(2) a. My dog is in the backyard.
b. There's milk in the glass.
c. The projector is on the table.
d. The screen is behind me.

Yet, just as it is possible to temporally anchor the spatial relations in (2), it is clear that language allows for events to be anchored in space with regularity (cf. (3)).

(3) a. The party was in the basement.
b. The committee held a vote in the conference room.
c. The dog walked on the carpet with his dirty paws.
d. Sophie danced in her bedroom.

Still, Vendler (1967) believed that the predicative operations involved in locating objects in space should not be associated with events. This "to each their own" philosophy forces the spatial properties of events (as well as the temporal aspects of objects) to be derivative in nature. We return to this below, with Davidson's ([6]) introduction of events as first-class objects in semantics.

Briefly, two approaches to temporal anchoring can be distinguished: (i) time as modality; and (i) the method of temporal arguments. For the former approach, a sentence such as *John was happy* is treated as a proposition scoped by an operator, P: $P(happy(john))$ ([25, 15, 22]). The method of temporal arguments reifies the temporal index which is used to anchor the evaluation of the proposition:

(4) $\exists t[hungry(john, t) \wedge t < now]$

This method was first explored in Russell [33] and Kim [17], but did not become common until McCarthy and Hayes [21] incorporated it into the situation calculus for automatic reasoning systems. By individuating the proposition as an event, Davidson's proposal is similar, in that it employs the "method of arguments" with an additional parameter, e.

The methods available for locating events in space are similar to those employed for time: namely, using a modality or adding an argument. Treating space as a modality has been explored since Rescher and Garson [32]. For example, to express the location in the sentence, *John met Mary*, a modal operator P_α can be employed, denoting, e.g., "some location other than here":

(5) $P_\alpha(meet(john, mary))$

The method of spatial arguments proposes a location argument to a relation, as shown below:

(6) $\exists l[meet(john, mary, l) \wedge in(l, \text{Boston})]$

This has been standard within situation calculus fragments for naive theories of physics (e.g., Hayes [10]), and is the starting point for defining topological relations within the qualitative spatial reasoning (QSR) community [30, 3] as well.

It is also the approach taken by Davidson [5] in his semantics of action sentences. Starting with the assumption that an event is a first-order individual, e, participating in the argument structure of a predicate, $P(x_1, \ldots, x_n, e)$, Davidson identifies the location of an event as a relation between the event variable and an introduced location argument, l, e.g., $loc(e, l)$. For example, consider the sentence and logical form below, ignoring for now, issues of tense.

(7) a. John sang in a field.
b. $\exists e \exists l[sing(j, e) \wedge in(e, l) \wedge field(l)]$

Regardless of the specific spatial relation present (*on*, *under*, *in back of*), Davidson's program is focused on relating the event to an object or location, rather than actually localizing the action itself. To illustrate this, consider the sentences in (8) and the predicated locations of the contained events.

(8) a. Mary ate her lunch under a bridge.
b. The robbery happened behind the building.

Notice that the events are positioned *relative* to the other objects and are not actually located *in* space.

Because of their grammatical and semantic import, linguistic interest in identifying the locations of events has focused largely on motion verbs and the role played by paths. Jackendoff [12, 14] elaborates a semantics for motion verbs incorporating explicit reference to the *path* traversed by the mover, from source to destination (goal) locations. Talmy's ([34, 35]) work develops a similar conceptual template, where the path followed by the figure is integral to the conceptualization of the motion event frame. Hence, the path can be identified as the central element in defining the location of the event. Related to this idea, both Zwarts [38] and Pustejovsky and Moszkowicz [29] develop mechanisms for dynamically creating the path traversed by a mover in a manner of motion predicate, such as *run* or *drive*. Starting with this approach, the localization of a motion event, therefore, is at least minimally associated with the path created by virtue of the activity.

In addition to capturing the spatial trace of the object in motion, several researchers have pointed out that identifying the shape of the path during motion is also critical for fully interpreting the semantics of movement. Eschenbach et al [8] discusses the orientation associated with the trajectory, something they refer to as *oriented curves*. Motivated more by linguistic considerations, Zwarts [39] introduces the notion of an *event shape*, which is the trajectory associated with an event in space represented by a path. He defines a shape function, which is a partial function assigning unique paths to those events involving motion or extension in physical space. This work suggests that the localization of an event makes reference to orientational as well as configurational factors. Zwarts also points out that the scalar semantics of degree predicates (such as *widen*) can be analyzed through the use of path composition rules [39], as well.

Beyond the work mentioned above, there has been little effort to articulate a general semantics for event localization that incorporates non-motion predicates. In this paper, I will propose some initial thoughts on what such a model should look like. The approach I take here is based on two distinct but interacting observations. First, I extend the path metaphor to non-movement events. This forces us to look at the various regions associated with the event participants, and the interactions between the participants. Secondly, I draw a distinction between the "relative spatial anchoring" of Davidson's analysis, and the actual event localization, which is the minimal location within which the action or event takes place. I argue that this is analogous to the distinction between an event's tense and its aspect within the temporal domain. On this view, Davidson's relative locational interpretation can be viewed as the reference location of the event, i.e., the *spatial aspect*. Similarly, the actual region encompassing the event is analogous to the tense (event time), and it is this region that we refer to as the *event locus*.

In the next section, we will see that the determination of the event locus is supervenient on the participants of the event, but not as transparently or predictably as might be expected.

3 A Procedure for Event Localization

As mentioned above, there are two observations that will be spelled out in this section: (i) the path metaphor can be extended to account for the localization of many non-movement activities; and (ii) event localization is formally analogous to grammatical tense, while spatial adjunction is analogous to grammatical aspect.

While Davidson's theory of action has had enormous influence on the way linguists and cognitive scientists approach the modification of events, including spatial predication, alternative views were voiced as early as Kim [18]. Motivated in large part by his theory of event identity, contra Davidson [6], Kim incorporated localization as an integral component to the definition of an event. Assume that an event is a structured object, exemplifying a property (or n-adic relation), at a time, t, as illustrated in (9).

(9) $[(x_1, \ldots, x_n, t), P^n]$

We can identify the location of an object in the event as: $loc(x, t) = r_x$. Then, for purposes of event identity, we can construe an event with its localization as:

(10) $[(x_1, \ldots, x_n, r_{x_1}, \ldots, r_{x_n}, t), P^n]$ or $=$ $[([x_i], [r_{x_i}], t), P^n]$

Accorindg to Kim [19], what we are calling the event localization, l_e, is supervenient on the object locations, $r_{x_1}, \ldots, r_{x_n}$, as defined above. This is a significant step beyond Davidson's approach since it introduces the supervenience of the event participants directly into consideration of the event location. However, since this problem was not as central to Kim's general program for defining property exemplication in the role of causation, this line of inquiry is not further developed in his or his colleagues' subsequent works, leaving most of our questions unanswered. First, how are the individual participant regions, x_i, composed or combined to create the proper minimum embedding space over the course of an event? Second, which participants are relevant in the composition of the embedding space for the event and which should be ignored? Finally, what happens when the participants to events are abstract objects or complex types? This is unfortunate, since this perspective on locating events merits further consideration.

The approach adopted by Zwarts [38, 39] can be seen as developing some of Kim's original insights into localization, as applied to movement predicates. Similarly, the generalization of the path metaphor, as taken up in [29, 20] can be viewed as essentially an extension of these ideas, as well. For the present discussion, we adopt the analysis given in [29] to introduce the localization of a motion event. First, we assume that path verbs such as *arrive* and *leave* are inherently different from basic manner-of-motion predicates, such as *move*, *roll*, and *walk*, in that they make explicit reference to the location that is being moved away from or toward along an explicit path, p. Manner verbs assume a change of location while making no explicit mention of a distinguished place. Path verbs can be identified as transitions, while manner-of-motion verbs can be seen as processes. Adopting the analysis of manner-of-motion predicates from [29], we say that a process "leaves a trail" as it is executed. For motion verbs such as *walk* or *run*, this trail is the created object of the path which the mover traverses. This argument is unexpressed in the syntax but present in the inspection of any state or trace of the process. Following [29], we treat the path as a program variable, $\hat{p}$, to the motion verb, dynamically creating the trail as an 'initiated" object from the resource locations, z, as illustrated below:

(11) a. **move**: $e_N \rightarrow (e_A \rightharpoonup (e_N \rightarrow s \times s))$
b. $\lambda z \lambda_{\rightharpoonup} \hat{p} \lambda x[walk(x, z, \hat{p})]$

We can identify the event localization for a motion predicate as the minimum embedding space, μ, for the moving object, x, traced over the course of the event. This includes both the path, $\hat{p}$, and the object localization for x, r_x. We denote this composition as $\hat{p} \otimes r_x$. For an event, e, with participants, x_i, the minimum embedding space can be computed, somewhat informally, as follows:

(12) a. r_{x_i}: The Kimian spatial extent of an object, x_i;
b. $\hat{p}$: The path created by the motion in e;
c. R_e: an embedding space (ES) for e, defined as a region containing $\hat{p}$ and r_{x_i} in a specific configuration, $\hat{p} \otimes r_{x_i}$;
d. μ, the event locus: the minimum embedding space for e.[1]

Now that we have established *where* a motion event is localized, i.e., its locus, we consider how a *reference location* can be introduced relative to the locus. As mentioned before, we refer to this region as the *spatial aspect* for the event, because it appears to function in much the same way as grammatical aspect in the temporal domain. Let us spell out this comparison. Tense is an ordered k-partitioning of the temporal domain, $\mathcal{D}_{\mathcal{T}}$; further, it is a nominal ordering (past, present, future). Now, grammatical aspect can be seen as a binary partitioning relative to this partition. This is one way of interpreting Reichenbach's (1947)

[1] Where μ can be defined as:
$\forall e \forall R_e \forall \mu[[ES(R_e, e) \wedge Min(\mu, R_e)] \leftrightarrow [\mu \subseteq R_e \wedge \forall y[y \subseteq R_e \rightarrow \mu \subseteq y]]]$.

calculus, utilizing Event (E), Reference (R), and Speech (S) times for classifying tense-aspect combinations in language [31]. To illustrate just part of this system, notice how Event and Reference times align to distinguish three relative orderings:

(13) a. Simple Past: $E = R$, $R < S$. John **ate**$_{E,R}$ dinner.
b. Past Perfect. $E < R$, $R < S$. John **had eaten**$_E$ dinner before noon$_R$.
c. Past Progressive: $R \subseteq E$, $E < S$. John [**was eating**$_E$]$_R$ dinner.

In a similar fashion, event localization as expressed in language can be seen as involving both an initial partitioning over the spatial domain, $\mathcal{D}_\mathcal{S}$, creating an event locus (l_e), as well as an optional subsequent partitioning relative to this partition, generating a spatial aspect (or reference location, l_r) [4]. Movement events provide a simple illustration of this process, since the locus is a fairly direct composition of the path $\hat{p}$ and the mover x, $\hat{p} \otimes r_{x_i}$.[2] There are two basic strategies available to motion verbs for referencing spatial regions pertaining to an event, and in the process create a partition relative to the locus. These are presented below in (14).

(14) a. ANALYTIC ASPECT: verb selects a spatial argument;
Mary left *the room.* John entered *the hall.*
b. SYNTHETIC ASPECT: verb is modified through PP adjunction;
Mary swam *in the pool.* John walked *to the corner.*

Path predicates that select a spatial sub-region of the locus as an argument are examples of the strategy in (14a) above, while both manner of motion and path predicates license PP adjunction in (14b). Some examples of how the locus is distinguished from spatial aspect are presented below.

(15) a. Simple Locus: $l_e = l_r$. John **walked**$_{l_e,l_r}$.
b. Relative Aspect: $l_e <_d l_r$. John **walked**$_{l_e}$ under the tree$_{l_r}$.
c. Embedded Aspect: $l_e \subseteq l_r$. John **walked**$_{l_e}$ in the building$_{l_r}$.
d. Completive Aspect: $\mathbf{EC}(l_e, l_r)$, $\mathbf{end}(l_r, \hat{p})$. John **arrived**$_{l_e}$ home$_{l_r}$.
John **walked**$_{l_e}$ to the park$_{l_r}$.[3]
e. Ingressive Aspect: $\mathbf{EC}(l_r, l_e)$, $\mathbf{begin}(l_r, \hat{p})$. John **walked**$_{l_e}$ from the park$_{l_r}$.

As pointed out in [29], we can characterize the locus as being *telic* or *atelic*, depending on the nature of $\hat{p}$ (which is dependent on the verb in composition with the PP).[4] In the next section we illustrate how the localization procedure extends to non-movement events.

[2] Support for this comes from a somewhat related analysis, where Reichenbach's reference frame for the temporal domain is extended to spatial frames of reference Tenbrink [36]. That analysis , however, does not extend to event localization.

[3] Spatial distinctions associated with *arrive* and *enter*, as well as *to* and *into* are acknowledged but not discussed in the present paper (cf. [12, 13, 23, 9, 39]).

[4] Besides the atelicity associated with source PPs, is the distinction between telic and atelic prepositions [38]: a. Mary swam *to* the beach; b. Mary swam *towards* the beach.

4 Non-Movement Event Localization

In this section, we briefly consider what is required to extend the localization procedure to non-movement events. The discussion will be somewhat programmatic in nature, due to space limitations. Since the path metaphor has already been applied to the semantics of creation and destruction predicates [27, 28] within the dynamic logic framework outlined in [29], we begin our discussion with this semantic class. On this view, verbs of change, such as *build*, *knit*, *destroy*, and *break*, can be seen as involving the creation or destruction of an object, seen as the *path* resulting from the event. For a verb such as *knit* (*John knitted a sweater.*), this path is the created object brought about by order-preserving transformations as executed in the directed process [28].

Thus, the event localization for creation predicates can be analyzed as the minimum embedding space for the created object traced over the course of the event, along with the other event participants. This is the created object as path, $\hat{p}$, in composition with the object localization of the agent argument, x, i.e., $\hat{p} \otimes r_x$. Applying this to other creation predicates, this also accounts for the dynamically changing spatial extent of a table or a house, as it is being constructed over a period of time (16).

(16) a. Simple Locus: $l_e = l_r$. John $\mathbf{built}_{l_e,l_r}$ a house$_{\hat{p}}$.
b. Embedded Aspect: $l_e \subseteq l_r$. John $\mathbf{built}_{l_e}$ a table$_{\hat{p}}$ in the basement$_{l_r}$.

Notice that in (16b), the locus of the building event is determined relative to the embedding reference location, l_r, making no commitment as to where the created object, $\hat{p}$, is located after the build event; e.g., the table may have gone into the kitchen when done.[5] Compare this to our interpretation of (17).

(17) John build a fence in the backyard.

The intented final placement of the created artifact is not captured by the event localization procedure, but is rather part of the world knowledge or qualia structure associated with the object [26].

One closely related verb class that should be briefly mentioned here is the class of *placement* predicates. These include verbs such as *put*, *place*, and *plant*. Notice that the localization of the event in (18) is similar to a path predicate, such as *enter*.

(18) Mary planted a tree in the ground.

Here, the locus is composed of the path, $\hat{p}$, taken by the plant, x, while the spatial aspect is an argument selected by the predicate, i.e., l_r is the ground, where $\mathbf{end}(l_r, \hat{p})$. The semantics of the predicate ensures the entailment $r_x \subseteq l_r$; the plant ends up "in" the ground.

One problem that arises with the procedure for event localization for causative predicates (such as the change predicates above) concerns the nature of the agent argument. Namely, when the causal argument is itself an event (or complex type), the supervenience strategy fails. Consider the following pair of sentences in (19).

[5] This is consistent with the syntactic attachment of the PP.

(19) a. Atelic Relative Aspect: $l_e <_d l_r$.
The storm **approached**$_{l_e}$ the shore$_{l_r}$.
b. Embedded Aspect with event agent: $l_e \subseteq l_r$.
The storm **destroyed**$_{l_e}$ the boat in the harbor$_{l_r}$.

While the sentence in (19a) treats the storm as a region in motion and has predictable event localization properties, the sentence in (19b) illustrates that the locus is not supervenient on the entire object localization of the causing argument (the storm), but of the local effects of this event: that is, the locus is restricted to within the harbor, $l_e \subseteq l_r$, where l_r is the harbor. This would no be possible if the locus were supervenient on the r_x associated with the storm, which would engulf the entire region. Notice that such a "locality" effect is also operative in other causative examples, such as that below:

(20) The sun killed the grass on the lawn.

With such cases, it appears that the effects of distal causation are computed locally (through a sort of transitivity operation), leaving the locus of the event to be proximate to the resulting state.

As our final verb class, we consider briefly perception predicates, such as *see* and *hear*. These pose a particularly interesting challenge to the procedure presented here because, following [11, 26], such verbs select for event complements. This introduces the problem of identifying two event distinct loci in a perception report. Consider the sentences below in (21).

(21) a. John saw an eagle in his backyard.
b. Mary heard an alarm down the street.

Following these analyses, we can distinguish the locality of the experiencing event from the event being perceived, where each seems to have a localization independent of the other. Hence, "the eagle in the backyard" is the event perceived by John, in his kitchen or wherever. Similar remarks hold for (21b), where the events have distinct loci. This is an area of considerable complexity, and merits further research, as the discussion here does it no justice.

5 Conclusion

In this brief note, I hope to have demonstrated that determining the location of an event is an area of research that has not been pursued as systematically as temporal localization of events or object localization. Contrary to a Davidsonian relativist view on localization, I introduce the distinction between an event's locus and its aspect, making an analogy to the distinction in the temporal domain between tense and aspect, or event and reference time. In the process, I have employed Kim's original notion of object supervenience to an extended path metaphor for the location of an event. Many issues remain to be addressed. One of the most significant gaps in the present analysis is the role of the *affordance space* associated with artifactual objects, in order to determine the appropriate region associated with the appropriate use of objects. Further examination is also required to clarify the role of locality in the broader class of causative predicates.

Acknowledgements

This research was supported by a grant from the NSF (NSF-IIS 1017765). I would like to thank Zachary Yochum and Marc Verhagen for their comments and discussion. All errors and mistakes are, of course, my own.

References

1. Bennett, B., Galton, A.: A unifying semantics for time and events. Arificial Intelligence 153, 13–48 (2004)
2. Chierchia, G.: Structured meanings, thematic roles, and control. Properties, types, and meaning 2, 131–166 (1988)
3. Cohn, A.G., Renz, J.: Qualitative spatial representation and reasoning 46, 1–2 (2001)
4. Coventry, K.: Saying, seeing and acting: The psychological semantics of spatial prepositions. Psychology Press (2004)
5. Davidson, D.: Intending. Essays on actions and events pp. 83–102 (1980)
6. Davidson, D.: The logical form of action sentences. Essays on actions and events 5, 105–148 (1967)
7. Egenhofer, M., Mark, D.: Modeling conceptual neighborhoods of topological line-region relations. International Journal of Geographical Information Systems 9(5), 555–565 (1995)
8. Eschenbach, C., Habel, C., Kulik, L., et al.: Representing simple trajectories as oriented curves. In: FLAIRS-99, Proceedings of the 12th International Florida AI Research Society Conference. pp. 431–436 (1999)
9. Galton, A.: Qualitative Spatial Change. Oxford University Press, Oxford (2000)
10. Hayes, P.J.: Naive physics I: Ontology for liquids. Morgan Kaufmann Publishers Inc. (1989)
11. Higginbotham, J.: The logic of perceptual reports: An extensional alternative to situation semantics. The Journal of Philosophy pp. 100–127 (1983)
12. Jackendoff, R.: Semantics and Cognition. MIT Press (1983)
13. Jackendoff, R.: Parts and boundaries. Cognition 41(1), 9–45 (1991)
14. Jackendoff, R.S.: Semantic structures, vol. 18. MIT press (1992)
15. Kamp, J.: Tense logic and the theory of linear order. s.n. (1968), http://books.google.com/books?id=FURDAAAAIAAJ
16. Kim, J.: Events as property exemplifications. Action theory pp. 159–177
17. Kim, J.: On the psycho-physical identity theory. American Philosophical Quarterly 3(3), 227–235 (1966)
18. Kim, J.: Events and their descriptions: some considerations. Essays in honor of Carl G. Hempel pp. 198–215 (1969)
19. Kim, J.: Causation, nomic subsumption, and the concept of event. The Journal of Philosophy pp. 217–236 (1973)
20. Mani, I., Pustejovsky, J.: Interpreting Motion: Grounded Representations for Spatial Language. Oxford University Press (2012)
21. McCarthy, J., Hayes, P.: Some philosophical problems from the standpoint of artificial intelligence. Stanford University (1968)
22. Montague, R.: The proper treatment of quantification in ordinary english. Approaches to natural language 49, 221–242 (1973)

23. Muller, P.: A qualitative theory of motion based on spatio-temporal primitives. In: Cohn, A.G., Schubert, L., Shapiro, S.C. (eds.) KR'98: Principles of Knowledge Representation and Reasoning, pp. 131–141. Morgan Kaufmann, San Francisco, California (1998)
24. Parsons, T.: Events in the Semantics of English. A Study in Subatomic Semantics. MIT Press, Cambridge, MA (1990)
25. Prior, A.: Time and modality. 1957. My present modification of the position there stated owes much to PT Geach's criticism in the Cambridge Review p. 543 (1957)
26. Pustejovsky, J.: The Generative Lexicon. Bradford Book, Mit Press (1995)
27. Pustejovsky, J., Jezek, E.: Scale shifting and compositionality. In: Proceedings of Scalarity in Verb-Based Constructions. Heinrich-Heine-Universität Düsseldorf, Germany (2011)
28. Pustejovsky, J., Jezek, E.: Verbal patterns of change. In: Osswald, R., Löbner, S. (eds.) Scalarity in Verb-Based Constructions. Oxford University Press (2013)
29. Pustejovsky, J., Moszkowicz, J.: The qualitative spatial dynamics of motion. The Journal of Spatial Cognition and Computation (2011)
30. Randell, D., Cui, Z., Cohn, A.: A spatial logic based on regions and connections. In: Kaufmann, M. (ed.) Proceedings of the 3rd Internation Conference on Knowledge Representation and REasoning. pp. 165–176. San Mateo (1992)
31. Reichenbach, H.: Symbolic logic. Berkeley: University of California (1947)
32. Rescher, N., Garson, J.: Topological logic. The Journal of Symbolic Logic 33(4), 537–548 (1968)
33. Russell, B.: The principles of mathematics. WW Norton & Company (1903)
34. Talmy, L.: How language structures space. In: Pick, H., Acredolo, L. (eds.) Spatial Orientation: Theory, Research, and Application. Plenum Press (1983)
35. Talmy, L.: Towards a cognitive semantics. MIT Press (2000)
36. Tenbrink, T.: Reference frames of space and time in language. Journal of Pragmatics 43(3), 704–722 (2011)
37. Vendler, Z.: Linguistics in philosophy. Cornell University Press Ithaca (1967)
38. Zwarts, J.: Prepositional aspect and the algebra of paths. Linguistics and Philosophy 28(6), 739–779 (2005)
39. Zwarts, J.: Event shape: Paths in the semantics of verbs (2006)

AUTHOR INDEX